The Plains tribes fought hard against white expansion. They were ironically aided by a European import: horses. Mounted on these swift animals, the tribes could fight and hunt much more effectively than they could on foot. But by the late 1870s, buffalo herds had been devastated by white hunters. The remaining Native Americans were forced onto **reservations,** pieces of land often far from their original homes.

Recent Native American history

In the second half of the 20th century, Native Americans began to gain a greater voice in North America. They protested and demonstrated in public to demand **redress** and acknowledgement of past wrongs.

Today, Native American populations have increased, tribes govern themselves, and artists continue to create both traditional and new works of art.

Native Americans often look to their past for guidance, but they also live very much in the present. Much of present-day Native American art may be rooted in past traditions, but it can be created using modern tools and techniques, reflecting the problems and triumphs of modern life.

Gerrit Greve painted *Native American War Bonnet* in 1975.

1960s: New activism in Native American communities leads to celebrations of culture and demonstrations against past wrongs

1990: The Native American Arts and Crafts Act of 1990 is passed in the United States and prohibits individuals from advertising art as Native American-made if it is not

2004: The National Museum of the American Indian opens on the National Mall in Washington, D.C.

Beliefs and Traditions

Despite different experiences and beliefs, Native American cultures share the view that all things, including trees, animals, and people, have a spirit. Native American artists take this spiritual dimension into account when they produce pieces of art.

The spirit world

Native American people have always been concerned about their relationship with the spirit world. They use ceremonies, **rituals**, and prayers to honor and make contact with spirits, to offer thanks, and to live a balanced, respectful life.

Native American art is often filled with images of animals and natural forces. These images call upon the spirits and make ordinary objects **sacred**. For example, hunters and warriors prayed for the power, strength, and speed of the buffalo. A painting of a buffalo could be a way of connecting with the buffalo's spirit, and a way to ask that spirit for help and protection. Some traditional Native American stories tell of how, in ancient times, humans and animals could change into each other at will. Humans often called upon their animal ancestors for aid or advice.

Traditionally, Native American history was told through dance, storytelling, and art. For example, this 19th-century blanket shows the Navajo **creation myth**, in which two sacred beings bring the gift of corn to the Navajo people.

Totem poles, made by the tribes of the northwestern United States and southwestern Canada, are tall structures carved from wood. Totem poles helped different **clans** tell the stories of their ancestors.

Many Native American rituals are a retelling of a sacred story. A ceremony with masks and figures might explain where people came from or how certain animals or plants became the main source of food for a tribe. The stories were also lessons that revealed how a person should act and advised which spirits were helpful and which should be feared.

Native American art helps bring ancient stories alive. For example, the thunderbird, a common image in Native American cultures, is said to cause thunder when it flaps its enormous wings. When it opens its eyes, jagged lightning flashes. Warriors would paint the thunderbird on their shields and garments, hoping that the power of the bird will come to their aid in battle.

Healing

Stories are also important in Native American healing ceremonies because they explain how a person received healing powers. During a ceremony these powers are called upon to heal a sick person. Masks, charms, and jewelry are used to draw upon the powers of the spirit world. Healers shake rattles and make paintings to satisfy or drive out the spirits that cause illness.

◇ Native American creation stories

Different Native American nations tell different **creation stories,** but some stories share common themes. One type of story, known as an earth diver story, describes the universe as first being a giant sea. Then a duck or other bird scrapes mud from the bottom of the ocean and puts the mud on the back of another animal, usually a turtle. The land grows and grows, becoming the Earth. Many Native American nations say that earthquakes come from the movements of the turtle.

Rock Art

Native Americans created designs, paintings, and carvings on rocks all over North America. It is estimated that there are at least 15,000 such sites. Some images show designs and shapes. Others depict people and animals. The images are either carved into the rock or painted using different colors. It can be difficult to date the images or to find out why they were made.

Coming of age

Some rock art has been linked to rites that mark a young person's coming of age. For example, in what is today British Columbia, Canada, young Native Americans went through an important **ritual** to become an adult.

Each boy went into the hills alone. After **fasting**, he prayed to a spirit for a vision that would become his guardian and helper for the rest of his life. The helper might be an animal, such as an eagle or a bear, or it could be a natural force, such as sunlight or thunder. After the boy's vision had occurred, he would go to a place among the rocks and paint the vision on a stone surface.

For a girl to become a woman, she was placed alone in a hut. There, she spent time in quiet **contemplation** and performed rituals of tasks that she would have to complete for the rest of her life. When she had finished, she painted images of these tasks on a rock.

Hunting

Rock art often depicted animals. The artists may have believed the images would help them attract and catch their prey. When depicting mythical beings, such as the water panther or the thunderbird, the hunter was requesting their aid.

Animal rock art is often found along major animal **migration** routes. Images of buffalo are located next to cliffs where hunters drove them to their deaths. Along the northwest coast, there are rock carvings of salmon, a common northwestern fish.

These two figures, which may represent spirits or ancestors, were probably carved into stone hundreds of years ago.

Historic events

Rock art also recorded important historic events. One example in the Canyon del Muerto in Arizona shows a figure on horseback with a cross. This symbolizes the arrival of the Spanish and their religion, Christianity.

The existence of rock art is very important for our understanding of history. While we have written accounts from the Spaniards describing their invasion of parts of North America, the rock art created by Native American people gives us a glimpse into how they themselves viewed the arrival of Europeans and the changing world around them.

◆ Cave paintings

Among the peaks of the Santa Ynez Mountains in present-day California, colorful paintings and designs cover the walls of a cave that was probably a **sacred** space. The images may have been painted by Native American medicine men as long as 400 years ago. Many of the designs are a mystery, but historians believe that one, a black circle outlined in a ring of blazing white, represents the solar **eclipse** that took place on November 24, 1677.

Chumash artists created detailed images for sacred spaces, such as the ones seen here in Chumash Cave in California.

This mask represents the mythical figure Bokwus, the Kwakiutl Wild Man of the Woods and chief of the dead. According to the myth, Bokwus lived in the forests of the northwest, feeding on rotten wood and grubs. He offered what appeared to be dried salmon to people. But after tasting the salmon, they died and joined his ghostly followers.

Masks from the northwest

When winter blanketed the northwest coast in freezing mists, the Tlingit tribe moved inland. They lived off stores of food that had been collected during the summer. It was a time for important ceremonies, dances, and festivals. Masks played an essential role.

In the flickering light of a lodge fire, masked dancers reenacted stories. Some recounted the stories of the **clan's** ancestors. Others depicted dark spirits engaged in evil or destructive actions, such as a sea monster that was said to cause floods and lead canoes astray. Other masks showed good spirits of people, animals, or nature.

The masks could be very dramatic and complex. Some could even be worked by strings, swinging open and shut to show the transformation of a person or spirit into an animal and back again. Other masks had several interchangeable mouthpieces that were designed to produce different sound effects and voices. Actors wore masks as they delivered their lines. These often included moveable features such as eyebrows and lips.

These ceremonies continue to be practiced in the northwest. Many historical masks have been saved and are still used today.

Kachinas

In the southwest, it is said that spirits called **kachinas** came out of the mountains every year to visit tribal peoples. Kachinas are spirits of rain, clouds, the dead, gods, and goddesses. There are several hundred kachinas in Pueblo culture. Some guarantee a safe home, others bring rain, and others promise a good crop. Some represent good or angry spirits, while others are simply clowns who entertain. Some kachinas are universal characters that are familiar to all Pueblo peoples, while others are only believed in by certain **clans.**

Each kachina has its own distinct mask. Native Americans dress in these masks and decorate their bodies to perform dances in underground chambers called **kivas**. In these ceremonies, the masks allow the spirits of the kachinas to enter the bodies of the dancers. Some kachinas bring medicine and healing powers, some control the seasons, and others bless new homes. This ensures that the powers of the spirits benefit the community for at least another year, at which time the ceremonies are repeated.

This kachina doll, created in the 1850s by a Hopi artist in the American southwest, represents a rain spirit. Rain was needed to grow corn. Here, the kachina's eyes depict clouds of rain and the eyelashes are raindrops.

Kachina dolls

Pueblo artists made kachina dolls for younger members of the tribe. These dolls were important learning tools. They were used to teach young Pueblos many complex stories of the kachina spirits and the traditions of their culture. Standing 6 to 12 inches (15 to 30 centimeters) tall, they are elaborately decorated and painted.

Today, Native American artists in the southwest continue to carve Kachina dolls. Their styles have evolved over time. Modern Native American artists usually carve the kachina from a single piece of wood, which they then decorate with paint, rather than making separate items for the doll to wear. The decoration of clothing takes its inspiration from modern society—some kachina dolls even wear T-shirts. Many people of different cultures are interested in these dolls, and they often sell for large sums of money.

These modern kachina dolls represent several characters and spirits. The headdresses, body paint, masks, and tools identify each individual kachina and its powers. These dolls were probably made to be sold.

Learning tools

Southwestern Native Americans protected their culture by not sharing many **artifacts** or stories about their ceremonies. Photographs of their rituals are rare, and they hardly ever allow someone from outside their village to observe **sacred** ceremonies in kivas. However, a little has been learned about kachina dress and ceremonies through kachina dolls.

Stone carving

Some Native Americans, notably those from the Hopewell culture in the eastern woodlands, considered stone carvings to be important enough to bury with their dead. Some tribes still follow this practice today. Most of the Hopewell carvings show animals taking part in a variety of activities. For example, one shows a bird spearing a fish with its beak, while another is in the shape of a beaver chipping away at a tree trunk. The carvings reveal not only artistic skill, but also a knowledge of how wild animals act. The carvings were done in a realistic manner to more effectively invoke the spirits to come to the aid of the dead person with whom they were buried.

The Inuit often made pipes from animal bone, covering them with designs and carvings of animals and people.

Pipe carving

The Hopewell people devoted enormous artistic energy to carving pipes from stone. Smoking was never done simply for pleasure. Tobacco was a highly valuable substance that was offered to the spirits and smoked at ceremonies. The wafting smoke was considered to unite the spirit world with the earthly world. Pipes were signs of peace and union with the spirit world and, as such, were covered with images reflecting this importance. Hopewell pipes were usually carved in the shape of an animal such as a frog, a hawk, or a panther. Freshwater pearls were often set into the head as eyes. Some rituals and ceremonies relied on the act of sharing a pipe in order to call on the spirit world.

The pipe was also extremely important among Plains tribes. There, pipes were considered not just a bridge to the spirit world, but also a link to past generations. According to Lakota teachings, the pipe was a gift from the Creator. It is said that a beautiful spirit named White

This Hopewell pipe, carved from stone around 400 B.C.E., was originally buried in a mound tomb. The Hopewell often carved animal shapes into their pipes.

Buffalo Calf Woman presented the pipe to the Lakota with these words:

"Behold this pipe! Remember always how **sacred** it is and treat it as such, for it will take you to the end. Remember, in me there are four ages. I am leaving but will look back on your people in every age, and in the end I will return."

Modern pipes

Native American artists continue to carve pipes to this day. White Buffalo Calf Woman's words have been remembered and the pipe is still seen in ceremonies among the Lakota and other tribes. The Plains Indians often decorate their pipes. Just as they cover clothing or shields with images, these tribes also use objects, such as pipes, to tell their own histories. The pipe makes the power of each group's images and objects come alive and enter the living world.

Pottery

Native American cultures throughout North America made pottery to store and cook food and to carry water. Some cultures decorated these pots or molded them into figures. The Mississippian cultures, for example, created several pots in the shape of human faces or figures. Wherever pottery was made, it was created from local clay, shaped by hand, and heated by fire until it became hard.

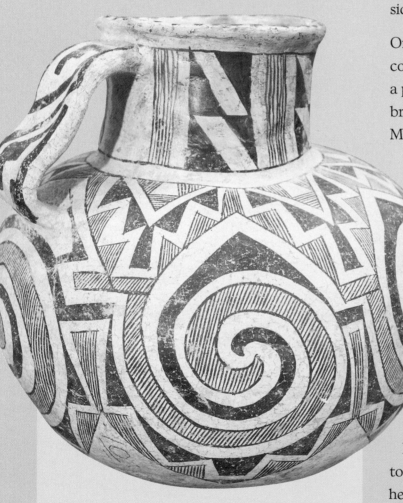

This water pitcher was created almost 1,000 years ago by the southwestern Mogollon culture. It is a fine example of the spiral paint patterns that the Mogollon favored.

Coil pots

The firing and painting of pottery flourished in the southwest, where techniques and patterns were passed from generation to generation for centuries. Native American potters in this area still use traditional materials and methods today. They dig clay from the local mesas, or plateaus. The clay is molded into long, flat tubes that are then coiled into the shape of a pot or bowl. The sides are then smoothed over.

Once a piece is formed, it is painted with natural colors. Black paint, for example, is made by boiling a plant called beeweed. The paint is applied with a brush made from the leaves of the yucca plant. Modern potters use a **kiln** to harden pots, but ancient potters set them over a fire made from goat dung. There was very little wood in the southwest. Goat dung was used because it heated quickly and evenly.

Mimbres pottery

The Mimbres culture, which flourished in the southwest between 1000 and 1200 C.E., produced pottery with painted designs. These designs mostly showed local animals, such as beetles, birds, jackrabbits, antelope, and coyotes.

In the Mimbres culture, it was traditional to put a pottery bowl with a hole in it over the head of a dead person and bury it with them. It was believed that the potter poured his or her soul into the bowl when he or she created it. By creating a hole in the bowl, the person's soul was free to join the dead on the journey to the afterlife.

This modern pot, made in the American southwest, is decorated with a bird design common to the Mimbres tradition.

Anasazi and Pueblo pottery

The Anasazi people, whose name means "enemy of our ancient ones," lived from about 1100 to 1450 C.E. in the southwest. They crafted bowls, drinking pots, and pitchers from clay, often decorating them with geometric black-and-white designs. When the Anasazi civilization broke apart and became Pueblo people, these Native Americans began to produce pottery decorated with colorful designs. By the 1880s the Pueblo tribes had become known around the world for their pottery.

Modern pottery

Pueblo pottery is still being produced today. In San Ildefonso Pueblo in New Mexico, a husband and wife developed a new way to decorate pottery. They packed each piece with cow dung and held it over a smoky fire. The result was a dark clay that could be decorated with a rich red color. They continued to produce this pottery throughout the 1970s.

Modern Native American artists

In 1990 the **Indian Arts and Crafts Board** was granted expanded powers of civil and criminal **jurisdiction** over **counterfeit** Native American arts and crafts. The Native American Arts and Crafts Act of 1990 made it illegal for anyone other than a Native American artist to advertise his or her artwork as being Native American, or as belonging to a particular tribe. This act helped establish a place in the art world for genuine Native American art—art that was born of and influenced by true Native American traditions.

Native Americans have sought to reconnect themselves with their past and use it to guide their lives. Many of these craftspeople use the techniques of their ancestors, although these are sometimes modified. For example, Bill Reid of the Haida tribe uses modern carving tools to depict the ancient stories of northwestern Native Americans. Norval Morrisseau of the Ojibwe tribe uses modern paints in his scenes of Native American culture. Rick Bartow of the Yurok tribe uses a variety of **media**, including printing, charcoal, and acrylic paints, to create colorful images of transformation. Kay Walkingstick of the Cherokee tribe paints images that incorporate historic Native Americans and the modern world.

The work of these artists and many others gives new life to some of the world's oldest and greatest artistic traditions. Today, the next generation of Native American artists is applying new artistic techniques to tribal histories, documenting the current link in the chain of Native American art and culture.

Today, many Native American artists use modern materials, such as the ink wash in this picture, to show traditional themes. This warrior was created by Gerrit Greve in 1976.

Glossary

abalone   type of mollusk whose shell is lined with mother of pearl, a shiny, multicolored substance favored in jewelry

abstract   art that uses shape, color, and pattern rather than specific images to communicate an artist's ideas

adapt   get used to something new, such as a climate, physical landscape, or culture

adobe   mud mixed with straw that forms a paste-like substance; this substance dries into a hard material that is used like a modern brick

agriculture   planting and raising of crops in an organized, planned manner

archaeologist   scientist who studies the physical remains of cultures

arid   dry; lacking water

artifact   object made by humans long ago

astronomical   having to do with the study of outer space and celestial bodies such as planets and stars

awls   small, pointed tools

cede   surrender possession of

clan   group of people within a larger tribe who are members of the same family

collage   combination of many shapes or images

collectively   as a group

colony   settlement of people who have come from another country to live in a new place

commemorate   honor with a ceremony

commission   place an order for, ask someone to create something (usually an artistic work)

contemplation   thoughtful study

counterfeit   object made to look like something else in an attempt to fool the viewer

coup   a blow or a strike; some tribes were known to "count coup," meaning to touch an enemy during battle to prove bravery

creation myths   stories that tell how each tribe came to be

creation stories   stories that explain the origins of each Native American group

dentalium shells   mollusk shells, often white and cone shaped

drought   long period of dryness that prevents the growth of crops

eclipse   blocking of the Sun's light by another body, such as a planet

extract   separate metal from ore

fasting   not eating food

game   wild animals hunted for food, such as buffalo

Ice Age   period of cold temperatures, when glaciers are present

igloo   structure made from large blocks of ice, usually used by northern tribes as a hunting base

Indian Arts and Crafts Board   a government agency created by the U.S. Congress to help Native American communities develop economically through arts and crafts marketing

indigenous   belonging to a place

inua   soul believed to exist in each person, animal, plant, lake, and mountain

irrigation   supply of water to dry land through a series of connected channels dug in the earth

jurisdiction   legal authority to control or make decisions about something

kachinas   spirits of Pueblo ancestors

kiln   oven used to bake and harden pottery

kiva   chamber in a Pueblo village used for ceremonies and meetings

loincloth   strip of cloth worn about a man's waist

loom   tool used to help weave fabric or thread

media   any material used in a work of art

mica   rock-forming mineral that flakes easily and was often used in Native American art

migration   mass movement of people or animals from one place to another, sometimes on a regular, seasonal basis

nomadic   describing people who have no fixed home and move about in search of food

octagon   eight-sided shape

oral tradition   passing of tribal histories and stories verbally from one generation to the next; a spoken, not written, history

ore   mineral containing metal

pelt   animal skin with the fur still attached

porcupine roaches   head ornaments made from porcupine hair and worn by male dancers

powwow   celebratory gathering of Native American tribes

Puritan   member of a group of English Protestants who moved to North America in the 17th century

redress   make amends for, set right

regalia   traditional clothing worn during ceremonies

reservations   pieces of land set aside by the U.S. government for Native Americans, often far from the tribes' original homes

rituals   religious ceremonies always performed in the same manner

sacred   relating to religious beliefs or practices

soldering   process of joining different pieces of metal by heating them

solstice   period when the sun is farthest away from the earth's equator. The solstice occurs twice a year, once in the summer and once in the winter.

tattoo   permanent pattern made by inserting a dye underneath human skin

teepee   portable living structure used by the Plains Indians and made from buffalo skins

totem poles   carved and painted cedar logs that tell the history of clans and their religious beliefs

trait   distinguishing feature

unprecedented   having never before happened

vision quest   act of seeking spiritual messages or guidance through isolated prayer and contemplation

Index

Since then, Andy slept with them both, one arm around each. Before he fell asleep, Andy talked to the quilted elephant about all the things they had done together. When he did that, the velvet dragon felt left out. But when Andy stroked the velvet dragon, the quilted elephant felt unwanted and sad.

During the day, when Andy was at school, the elephant and the dragon never spoke to each other. The dragon tried once or twice, but the elephant was always asleep, or pretending to be.

Every afternoon, when Andy came home, he played
with them both. But one afternoon, Andy didn't play with
either of them. Instead, he started pulling things out of his
dresser drawers.

"Something's happening!" said the dragon to the elephant. "Look! What's Andy up to?"

"Oh, my," said the elephant. "He's packing. That means he's going to sleep over."

"Will he take us?" asked the dragon.

"Well, I'm sure he'll take *me*. He always has. But there won't be room in his duffle for both of us."

"Then he'll take *me*, not *you*," said the dragon. "Your seams are split, and your stuffing is coming out."

"That's because he's played with me longer. I'm his oldest friend. He'll certainly take *me*."

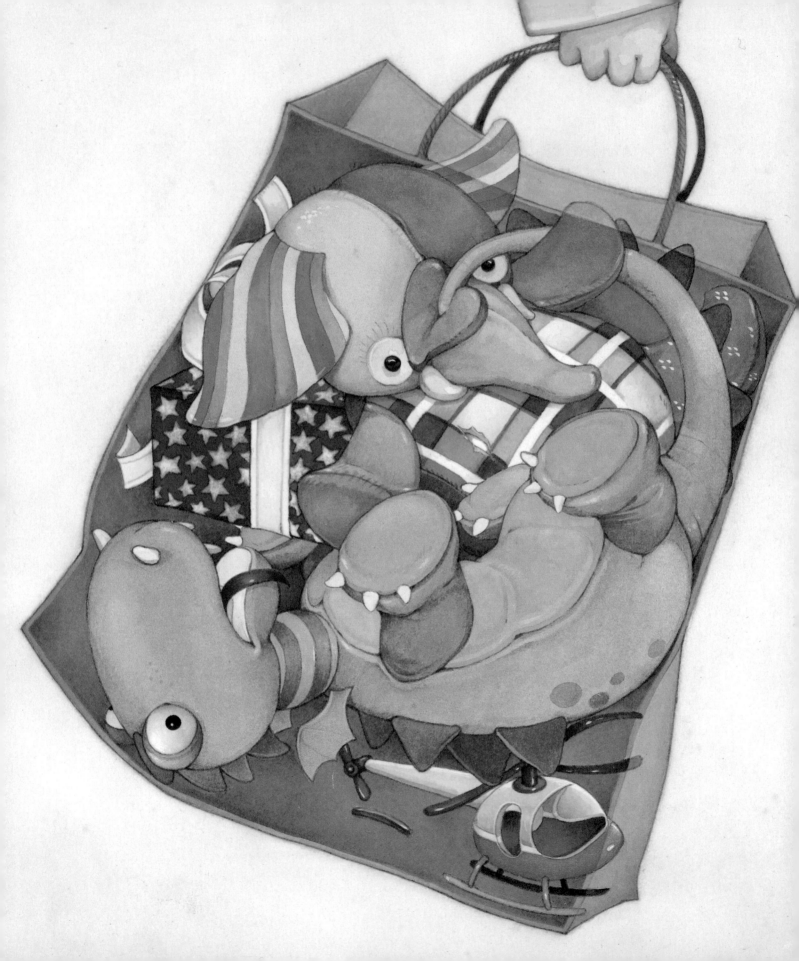

Andy came back in. He picked up the velvet dragon and hugged him. The dragon wanted to throw his paws around Andy and give him a dragon hug. But of course he couldn't.

Then Andy picked up the quilted elephant. The elephant wanted to curl her trunk around Andy and give him an elephant hug. But of course she couldn't.

"I don't know which one of you to choose," said Andy. "Maybe I can take you both."

"Uh-oh, there isn't room for either one of you. I know— maybe you'll both fit in the shopping bag with the present for Kevin."

"Oh, good, there *is* room, and for some toys, too."

"Oh, dear," said the dragon. "That box is going to poke a hole in my side."

"I don't mind being poked," said the elephant. "I'm full of holes already."

"It's awfully bumpy in here," said the dragon.

"It doesn't bother *me*," said the elephant. "I'm used to being tossed about."

"How far is he taking us?" asked the dragon.

"Only next door," said the elephant. "Now calm down."

"It's dark in here," said the dragon. "I'm afraid of the dark, unless I'm with Andy. He's forgotten all about us now that he has Kevin."

"Stop complaining," said the elephant. "At least we have more room in here now. I'll just have a little snooze until Andy comes to get us."

But the dragon stayed awake, thinking. If only one of them had fit in Andy's bag, which one would he have picked? And would Andy still love him if he *did* have a hole in his side?

He heard a noise—CLUNK-CLUNK-CLUNK. Then he heard a whirring sound. And then he heard Andy yell, "Let *me* do it."

BUMP! The elephant woke up. The dragon fell on his side. They felt fingers poking them as Andy went through his bag.

"I'll trade for this," Andy said.

"One of the rotor blades is missing," said Kevin. "What else did you bring?"

"He can walk on slanted places," said Andy.

"Wham!" said Kevin. "He fell on his head."

Kevin made the wooden man fall down over and over again.

"So you'll trade?" asked Andy.

"I don't know," answered Kevin. "It's fun for a while, but then it gets boring. What else did you bring?"

"I didn't bring any other toys," said Andy.

"There's something else in that bag. I can tell," said Kevin.

The elephant and dragon lay there, frightened.

"These aren't toys," said Andy. "They're just my stuffed animals."

"Do they make noises if you squeeze them?" asked Kevin.

"No. But the dragon's tongue comes out. Watch!" Andy squeezed the dragon and went R-R-ROARRR!

"That's neat," said Kevin. He kept squeezing the dragon and running around with him, roaring. The dragon didn't like it. Kevin squeezed him too hard.

RAINTREE BIOGRAPHIES

Frank Lloyd Wright

Scott Ingram

Published by Raintree, a division of Reed Elsevier, Inc.

Project Editors: Marta Segal Block, Helena Attlee
Production Manager: Brian Suderski
Designed by Ian Winton

Planned and produced by Discovery Books

Library of Congress Cataloging-in-Publication Data:

Ingram, Scott (William Scott)
Frank Lloyd Wright / Scott Ingram.
p. cm. -- (Raintree biographies)
Summary: A biography of the innovative American architect
whose ideas influenced the direction of design in the twentieth century.
Includes bibliographical references and index.
ISBN 0-7398-6866-7 (HC), 1-4109-0068-1 (Pbk.)
1. Wright, Frank Lloyd, 1867-1959--Juvenile literature.   2. Ar-
chitects--United States--Biography--Juvenile literature.   [1.
Wright, Frank Lloyd, 1867-1959. 2. Architects.]   I. Title. II. Series.
NA737.W7I54 2003
720'.92--dc21
[B]

2002154987

Printed and bound in the United States
1 2 3 4 5 6 7 8 9 0 08 07 06 05 04 03

Acknowledgments
The publishers would like to thank the following for permission to reproduce their pictures:
Corbis: 8, 9, 10, 12, 14, 15, 19, 24, 26, 27, 28, 29; The Frank Lloyd Wright Foundation: 6, 7, 21;
The Hulton Archive: cover, 5, 18, 22; Jeffery Howe, Boston College: 4, 11, 13, 16, 17, 20, 23, 25.

Some words are shown in bold, **like this**.
You can find out what they mean by looking in the glossary.

CONTENTS

CHILDHOOD ON THE PRAIRIE

Frank Lloyd Wright was born on June 8, 1867, in the small farming town of Richland Center, Wisconsin. His father was a minister and a musician, and his mother a teacher.

Wright grew up surrounded by uncles, aunts, and cousins. This is a picture of his mother's family, the Lloyds.

Taliesin

Wright's grandparents came to Wisconsin from Wales, a part of Britain, during the 1860s. They settled about 40 miles (65 kilometers) west of Madison, where the steep hills rose from the flat land, reminding them of their homeland. They named the largest hill "Taliesin," the name of a famous Welsh poet. As a boy, Wright spent happy summers working at his uncle's farm, near Taliesin.

Wright's mother wanted her son to be an **architect** when he grew up and **design** buildings for a living. She hung pictures of some of the world's most famous buildings in his nursery. As soon as he could hold a pencil, he was taught to draw shapes such as circles, squares, and triangles. His mother also filled his playroom with glue and cardboard, so that he could make imaginary buildings.

When Wright was thirteen, the family settled in the town of Madison, Wisconsin, where he attended high school. At age fifteen, he was accepted as a student at the University of Wisconsin. A short time later, Wright's parents divorced, and he never saw his father again.

Frank Lloyd Wright never lost his love of the land. As an elderly man, he continued to work on the farm at Taliesin.

YOUNG ARCHITECT

In 1887, twenty-year-old Wright left college to become an architect. He moved to Chicago, Illinois, and soon found a job working for Louis Sullivan, one of the most famous architects in the United States. Sullivan's buildings in downtown Chicago were widely admired as some of the best examples of a new **structure** called a "**skyscraper**."

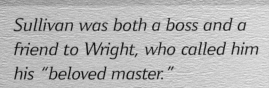

Sullivan was both a boss and a friend to Wright, who called him his "beloved master."

Rebuilding Chicago

In the mid-1800s, Chicago was a wealthy place. In 1871, however, a huge fire killed 300 people and destroyed thousands of buildings. This **tragedy** drew architects such as Louis Sullivan to Chicago, where they worked to rebuild the city. By 1890, there were dozens of new skyscrapers.

Wright quickly became Sullivan's chief **draftsperson**. He completed Sullivan's plans for stores, office buildings, and **auditoriums**, calling himself "the pencil in Sullivan's hands."

After several years, Sullivan put Wright in charge of his company's home **design** department. Soon, Wright began to develop ideas unlike any Sullivan had ever seen. The houses had low roofs, open rooms flowing into one another, and a fireplace in the center of the home. Sullivan soon asked Wright to design a home for his own family.

Sullivan's Auditorium Building had an open-air room at its center. It was considered one of the most beautiful buildings in Chicago.

THE BOOTLEG HOMES

By age 25, Wright was chief **architect** at Sullivan and Adler, the largest architectural company in Chicago. Wright was soon well known. Many people admired his work and asked him to **design** houses for them. Taking on work outside the company was called "bootlegging," and it was against the rules, but Wright had debts to pay. He took on private jobs, and was fired as a result.

These crowded Chicago streets, photographed at the beginning of the twentieth century, would have been familiar to Frank Lloyd Wright.

Regrets

In later years, Wright regretted the loss of his friendship with Sullivan, the man who had trained him in the basic ideas of **architecture**. *"The bad end to a glorious relationship,"* Wright wrote, *"has been a dark shadow . . . all the days of my life."*

Three Bootleg houses that Wright designed while working for Sullivan still stand in Oak Park. This is Walter Gale House, built in 1893.

Three of the houses that Wright designed while he was working for Sullivan and Adler can still be seen today in Oak Park, Illinois, a wealthy suburb of Chicago. By looking at them, we can understand Wright's first ideas about the design of houses. Some features of the Bootleg homes were completely new. For example, they had round front rooms and very long chimneys.

THE PRAIRIE STYLE

After he was fired, Wright set up an office in his home in Oak Park, Illinois. The house is now a museum that is visited by thousands of tourists each year. From 1893 to 1901, more than 40 Wright houses were built there in an original **design** that came to be known as his **Prairie** Style.

Wright experimented with many of his own ideas when building this house for himself in Oak Park.

Until Wright began to design houses, most buildings had tended to stand out from their surroundings. The Prairie homes were different. With their low, overhanging roofs and rows of small windows, the houses blended in with the **landscape**.

The inside of Wright's Prairie Style houses was also designed in a new way. Instead of breaking up the space into the usual small, boxes, he used glass doors between the rooms, and joined them around a central fireplace. Chairs, sofas, and tables were built out from the wall, so that much of the floor area was open and seemed larger than it was.

An example of Wright's Prairie Style, Nathan Moore House was built in Oak Park in 1895, and rebuilt in 1924.

GLOSSARY

architect person who designs houses or other buildings

architecture process of designing buildings

auditorium room or building used for public gatherings

autobiography story of someone's own life

cement mixture of lime and clay used in building

client person who buys or uses the services of another

concrete strong building material made by mixing cement with sand or gravel

craft job that needs skill, especially with the hands

craftsperson person who is especially skilled at a craft

design to create or construct. The plan for an object or building is called a design.

development an area of land used for building houses, stores, factories, etc.

draftsperson person who draws plans and sketches

facade front of a building

foundation base which supports a structure built above it

genius somebody with exceptional talent

landscape scenery or natural surroundings

legacy something handed down by a previous generation

masterpiece work or high achievement created with great skill

portfolio collection of work

prairie flat grassland with few trees or other plants

resort place where people go on vacatiion

skyscraper very tall, narrow building

streamlined having a smooth shape

structure something that has been constructed, such as a building

tragedy disastrous event

FURTHER READING

Boulton, Alexander O. *Frank Lloyd Wright Architect: A Picture Biography.* New York: Rizzoli International Publications, 1993.

Rubin, Goldman, Susan. *There Goes the Neighborhood: 10 Buildings People Loved to Hate.* New York: Holiday House, 2001.

Wilkinson, Philip. *Building.* New York: Dorling Kindersley Publishing, 2000.

INDEX

Numbers in *italics* indicate pictures